-Ele... English ... ...on Topics-

English for Elementary Level Students

Engaging ESL Activities to Develop Vocab, Confidence and Basic Conversational Skills

First published in 2019. All rights reserved

By Nigel M Openshaw

Copyright © Nigel M Openshaw

Table of Contents

Dedication

My true education as a teacher came from the students I taught in South Korea. I met some wonderful and truly inspirational people. Those students changed my outlook and vision of teaching to such an extent that now I am in a different frame of mind. To those students, to say thank you is simply not enough as they are almost like family. They will always be special to me.

Truly, thank you, Korea.

Preface

One day I looked at the teaching materials I'd accumulated as an ESL teacher in South Korea and realized what a great resource they'd make for other teachers.

The lessons collected in this book encouraged my students to speak English without causing the students to feel embarrassed about making mistakes. They were so much fun that I thought it would be great to share them with others.

This book helps build students' confidence by developing their English skills and increasing their vocabulary using a range of fun and motivating activities.

What is an ESL Teacher?

Over time, the traditional term ESL teacher has been replaced by the term experienced speaker. For students, ESL teachers are people with whom they can practice speaking and who can boost their confidence. The traditional form of teaching has evolved into edutainment.

When a student takes a lesson, they want to walk away with a good experience. For this to happen, they need to be immersed in an English environment that is both comfortable and informal.

A more relaxed learning environment helps soften the rigid boundaries between using English in and outside the classroom. This can be further improved by building trust and friendship in the lessons.

Control the Flow

When a lesson goes well, students will be doing most of the talking. The ESL teacher acts as a referee to share speaking roles and control the balance of speakers within the room.

Encourage open questions only, with no yes or no answers. It's OK to ignore students' mistakes if they are minor, but major errors should be corrected. For me, this would include errors in tenses and pronouns.

Language Differences

If the students are from various countries, then there may be some cultural differences and educational methods to deal with.

In theory, this situation can create a positive and supportive learning environment in which everyone listens to and tries to understand other people's languages and perspectives.

Students have many personal experiences and abilities that they can bring to the lesson. Teachers can make use of these experiences to develop and enhance classroom interactions.

When I was teaching English in South Korea, I saw many spontaneous interactions between students develop during lessons. If students speak together in English, I would encourage the students to talk even if they are not keeping strictly to the topic.

Don't Forget Other ESL Teachers

It can be tough for ESL speakers to go to another country and to adapt to a different culture. It can take many years to understand the language and customs of local people. I have known some ESL teachers who expected too much and were overly controlling as they were back home. This only resulted in losing the attention of a classroom of students as well as alienating the country's native teachers.

Understanding Students' Needs

Lessons generally have to be highly productive, especially for demanding students. To achieve that productivity, teachers have to find individual students' level of ability. Knowing what they can and cannot do gives the teacher control over how far to push students and in which directions.

This can be much harder as class size increases, so don't worry if getting to know students takes time. Eventually, you will become familiar with individual students' backgrounds and preferences. Teachers need to appeal to students' individual learning styles as this will help develop trust and bonding within the group.

Many English-language learners see the teacher and other class members as friends. Sometimes that can mean studying takes second place. If that is their goal, so be it. Remember, though, that the teacher can be moderated by students' grades and percentage of passes. So keep an eye on the main focus of the lessons; it's not only about establishing friendships.

My Experience

I am a qualified ESL teacher with TESOL certifications. I taught in South Korea for eight years before returning to Manchester, UK, where I have continued teaching ESL to students including Spanish and Arabic speakers.

Your Experience

I hope the methods and materials presented here give you as much fun and insight as they gave me and my students. I learned so much from the students diverse backgrounds that I would never have experienced without the opportunity of teaching abroad.

I would love to know about your experiences with these lessons. It would be great if you could give a review on Amazon and share the good vibes.

Introduction

The lessons that follow can be adapted to run from 30 to 90 minutes. They often start with about 5-10 minutes of free talking. This can cover how the students are, what they have been doing or plan to do, as well as contributions from the teacher.

The structure of the lessons is modular, with clear and obvious steps to take. Everything starts with the teacher's preparation work. Depending on the students' ability, topics might need a quick worksheet or short classroom activity at the start of the lesson, and you will need to set aside time to devise this.

The purpose of each lesson is for students to gain confidence and increase their vocabulary by talking about different topics. If they are unsure about what to do, this might mean introductory work is needed first.

Styles

Lessons always progress according to the following stages:

1. Warm-up and Objective - Introduce the topic and go over any preliminary exercises that need to be covered.
2. Exploration and Comprehension - Explain the class material and ensure students understand what has to be done.
3. Guided Student Practical - With help from the teacher, students practice the exercise in pairs or small groups.
4. Student Presentation and Evaluation - This is the students' opportunity to demonstrate to the rest of the class what they have discussed.
5. Review and Assess - At this stage, the teacher reviews any problems with comprehension and practical usage.
6. Bonus Activity - This could be a short but fun activity that acts as a method of review.

Topics

There are three lesson plans in this book. This doesn't mean this book is easy, but the focus should be on getting students talking.

Lesson 1 Keyword Discussions

This lesson is a brainstorming session as students think of words, including adjectives to describe a particular topic. Students need to understand keywords connected with a topic.

Lesson 2 Conversation Starters

This lesson introduces ways to begin and carry on a conversation. The lesson is designed to help guide students in a structured way in generating conversation ideas.

Lesson 3 Expanding Vocabulary

This lesson focuses on expanding vocabulary with synonyms and antonyms. This is a fun lesson that encourages open speaking and explores the use of verbs in depth. This is then used to build dialogue with simple questions and answers.

Materials

There is a list of reference materials to be used with each lesson. Please note that both British and US spellings of words are given, for example, "favourite/favorite."

Classroom Conditions

I have taught classes with anything up to twenty students using these materials. The lessons are easy to adapt depending on your classroom size and level. With a large class you can encourage smaller groups to discuss topics together and then ask students to share their ideas with the whole class.

Be aware of students' sensitivities. Some students may be a little nervous about expressing their opinions and emotions in front of the class. However, over time, they will come to realize that everyone else feels the same and their confidence will improve.

Keyword Discussions

Purpose

This lesson is a brainstorming session as students think of words, including adjectives to describe a particular topic. Students need to understand keywords connected with a topic.

Example

Celebrations: Birthday, party, wedding, graduation, Christmas and New Year

Lesson

Objectives

1. To expand vocabulary and brainstorm around a specific topic.
2. To continue and talk spontaneously about new topics.

Teacher Preparation

1. Choose a topic from References at the end of this lesson, for example, "Celebrations: Birthday, party, wedding, graduation, Christmas and New Year."
2. Take an A4 sheet of paper, turn it horizontally and draw six oval shapes (two rows of three ovals). In each of the ovals, write one word. Use any order to suit your needs.
3. If students don't know adjectives, devise a brief activity to explain.

Class Work

1. Warm-up and Objective

- Introduce the main topic of the lesson chosen in teacher's preparation work.

- Talk about adjectives if students are unfamiliar with this term.
- Talk about the final goal of the lesson: students will learn to have a controlled discussion about a given topic using a range of new vocabulary.

2. Exploration and Comprehension

- First, write the topic at the top of the board and ask students what it means.
- On the far right side of the board, write any words suggested by students that could be useful.
- Next, copy the template with the six main words onto the board for everyone to see.
- Go through the words one by one for comprehension checking. At this point, reintroduce any words students gave previously that are similar.
- Remember, this is only the introduction to the words and more will follow.

3. Guided Student Practical

- Divide the class into pairs or teams depending on the class size - the aim is to create discussion between students.

- Hand out the paper made in teacher's preparation work.
- Students write next to one of the six words any related words.
- Ask questions about the words for clarity and comprehension.
- Introduce adjectives to help in clarifying.
- Ask to use these words in spoken sentences to show if the students understand them and demonstrate their range of vocabulary.

4. Student Presentation and Evaluation

- This lesson is a continuous evaluation of students' understanding of the words given.
- Expansion of the topic into new areas is fine as long as students keep talking.

5. Review and Assess

- To wrap up, discuss the words covered as well as the main topic.
- Ask again for adjectives. Mix up the words to test clarity. Making negative questions will test students' comprehension.

Bonus Activity

The Word Competition

- As a bonus to this lesson, create a word league with other teams or classes.
- Each team or class has to write as many words as they can about the topic. This is simply a brainstorming session.
- Let each team know that their words will be turned into points.
- Record how many words each team or class comes up with and award prizes for the highest number.
- Proofing the words is essential as some may use words that don't fit.
- For the competition, introduce a new topic that hasn't been covered in class yet.

References

Below are groups of six words around a topic that students will talk about and brainstorm. The lists vary in elementary level topics. Initially is a list of adjectives and the order that they should be used.

Animals (Birds)

- Partridge, Crow, Chick, Duck, Duckling, Seagull
- Sparrow, Swallow, Gosling, Quail, Puffin, Albatross
- Hawk, Heron, Goose, Pelican, Pheasant, Eagle
- Peacock, Ostrich, Swan, Turkey, Vulture, Magpie

Animals (Pets, Fish and Sea Creatures)

- Bird, Cat, Chicken, Dog, Goldfish, Hamster
- Horse, Gerbil, Pigeon, Rabbit, Snake, Turtle
- Cod, Crab, Octopus, Lobster, Oyster, Salmon
- Sardine, Shark, Shrimp, Trout, Tuna, Squid

Animals (Farm and Insects)

- Calf, Cat, Chicken, Cow, Duck, Goat
- Hen, Horse, Lamb, Pig, Rooster, Sheep
- Ant, Bee, Beetle, Butterfly, Cockroach, Cricket
- Dragonfly, Ladybug, Mosquito, Moth, Bug, Spider

Animals (General)

- Badger, Beaver, Anteater, Hyena, Lion, Monkey
- Ostrich, Jaguar, Leopard, Snake, Tiger, Wolf
- Alligator, Zebra, Bear, Kangaroo, Camel, Cheetah
- Crocodile, Elephant, Giraffe, Gorilla, Panda, Rhinoceros

Body (Face and Upper Body)

- Tongue, Tooth, Nose, Eye, Face, Lip
- Mouth, Brain, Cheek, Chin, Ear, Hair
- Throat, Neck, Head, Heart, Shoulder, Lungs
- Wrist, Finger, Hand, Arm, Nail, Elbow

Body (Lower Body and Body Injuries)

- Chest, Toe, Feet, Ankle, Foot, Hip
- Knee, Leg, Muscle, Skin, Stomach, Back
- Black Eye, Blister, Broken Bone, Bruise, Burn, Cut
- Fracture, Lump, Scratch, Sprain, Sunburn, Swelling

Clothes

- Cap, Coat, Dress, Blouse, Gloves, Hat
- Jacket, Scarf, Shirt, Sweater, Tie, Vest
- Shoes, Shorts, Skirt, Slippers, Socks, Belt
- Boots, Jeans, Pyjamas/Pajamas, Trousers/Pants, Suit, Handkerchief

Countries

- Argentina, Australia, Austria, Belgium, Brazil, Canada
- China, Denmark, Finland, France, Germany, Greece
- India, Israel, Japan, Mexico, Philippines, Russia
- Singapore, South Korea, Spain, Sweden, United Kingdom, United States

House (General)

- Bathroom, Bedroom, Ceiling, Dining Room, Door, Floor
- Ground, Hall, Kitchen, Living Room, Wall, Bath Tub
- Bed, Chair, Furniture, Lamp, Picture, Shelf
- Sink, Sofa, Table, Toilet, Window, Garden

House (Bathroom)

- Bath, Shower, Sink, Cleaning, Tap/Faucet, Hand Towel
- Laundry Basket, Mirror, Waste Basket, Toilet, Scale, Disinfectant
- Brush, Scissors, Shampoo, Bubble Bath, Comb, Soap
- Sponge, Toothbrush, Toothpaste, Towel, Razor, Flannel

Foods (Fruit)

- Cherry, Blackberry, Blueberry, Clementine, Grapes, Tangerine
- Nectarine, Persimmon, Plum, Pomegranate, Raspberry, Strawberry
- Melon, Orange, Peach, Pear, Apple, Apricot
- Banana, Kiwi, Lemon, Lime, Pineapple, Watermelon

Foods (Desserts and Drinks)

- Apple Pie, Birthday Cake, Cake, Candy, Chocolate, Cookies
- Doughnuts/Donuts, Ice Cream, Muffin, Pie, Cheesecake, Pudding
- Cocoa, Coffee, Green Tea, Ice Coffee, Ice Tea, Juice
- Lemonade, Milk, Milkshake, Orange Juice, Soda, Tomato Juice

Foods (General)

- Bacon, Beef, Chicken, Ham, Heart, Kidney
- Lamb, Mutton, Pork, Steak, Turkey, Veal
- Bread, Cheese, Egg, Fish, Noodles, Pancakes
- Pasta, Peanuts, Rice, Cream, Milk, Yoghurt/Yogurt

Foods (Vegetables)

- Beans, Carrot, Corn, Cucumber, Courgette/Zucchini, Bell Pepper
- Onion, Peas, Tomatoes, Olives, Mushrooms, Beetroot
- Lettuce, Broccoli, Sprouts, Cabbage, Cauliflower, Celery

- Potato, Pumpkin, Radish, Spinach, Sweet Potato, Turnip

Jobs

- Dentist, Actor, Athlete, Doctor, Farmer, Fire Fighter
- Fisherman, Musician, Nurse, Pilot, Soldier, Teacher
- Engineer, Banker, Barber, Chef, Coach, Lawyer
- Mechanic, Police Officer, Priest, Professor, Veterinarian, Waiter/Waitress

Nature

- Cave, Desert, Mountain, Earth, Forest, Hill
- Seed, Nest, Swamp, Valley, Tree, Waterfall
- Bay, Beach, Pond, Creek, Island, Lake
- River, Riverbed, Sea, Stream, Ocean, Sand

People (Family)

- Aunt, Brother, Cousin, Daughter, Father, Mother
- Nephew, Niece, Parents, Sister, Son, Uncle
- Brother-in-Law, Father-in-Law, Grandson, Grandfather, Great Grandfather, Grandparents

•Sister-in-Law, Mother-in-Law, Granddaughter, Grandmother, Great Grandmother, Grandchildren

People (General)

- Sister, Brother, Boy, Girl, Woman, Man
- Baby, Toddler, Children, Teenager, Adult, Kid
- Classmate, Clerk, Customer, Enemy, Family, Friend
- Roommate, Best Friend, Stranger, Relative, Neighbour/Neighbor, Ancestor

School (Subjects)

- Geography, Art, History, Maths/Math, Music, Cooking
- Craft, Drama, Drawing, English, Games, Archaeology/Archeology
- Biology, Chemistry, Health, Chinese, Korean, Performing Arts
- Computer Science, Physics, Science, Sewing, Social Studies

School (Classroom)

- Blackboard, Notebooks, Desk, Chair, Calendar, Clock

- Computer, Plants, Drawings, Dictionary, Students, Teacher
- Chalk, Paper, Pens, Pencils, Pencil Case, Sharpener
- Textbook, Colour/Color Pens, Eraser, Reading Books, Bag, Homework

School (Books and Shapes)

- Book, Booklet, Brochure, Comic Book, Dictionary, Encyclopaedia/Encyclopedia
- Hardcover, Magazine, Novel, Paperback, Leaflet, Picture Book
- Circle, Cone, Cylinder, Hexagon, Oval, Pentagon
- Pyramid, Rectangle, Sphere, Square, Star, Triangle

Transportation and Vehicles

- Bicycle, Canoe, Kayak, Motorboat, Motorcycle, Horse
- Scooter, Police Car, Car, Glider, Taxi, Yacht
- Bus, Plane, Ambulance, Jet, Subway, Fighter Jet
- Fire Engine, Train, Truck, Helicopter, Submarine, Hovercraft

Town or City Buildings

- Airport, Bakery, Bank, Barber Shop, Book Store, Church
- Coffee Shop, Department Store, Petrol/Gas Station, Hospital, School, Shopping Mall
- Library, Theatre/Theater, Museum, Post Office, Restaurant, Supermarket
- Train Station, Fire Station, Police Station, Hotel, Fast Food Restaurant, Medical Clinic

Weather Conditions and Seasons

- Sun, Rain, Snow, Cloud, Part Sun and Cloud, Wind
- Thunder, Lightning, Fog and Mist, Hail, Shower, Rainbow
- Humid, Dry, Frost, Ice, Typhoon, Tornado
- Spring, Summer, Autumn/Fall, Winter, Temperature, Thermometer

Conversation Starters

Purpose

This lesson introduces ways to begin and carry on a conversation. The lesson is designed to help guide students in a structured way in generating conversation ideas.

Example

Hobbies: Shopping - Where do you go shopping? If you were rich, what would you buy? What snacks do you like to buy? Do you look for bargains?

Lesson

Objectives

1. To have a conversation using open questions.
2. To create sentences with specific words, including using the main question forms (5W+H).

Teacher Preparation

1. Choose a topic from References at the end of this lesson, for example, "Hobbies: Shopping - Where do you go shopping? If you were rich, what would you buy? What snacks do you like to buy? Do you look for bargains?"
2. If students are unfamiliar with the 5W+H (who, what, where, why, when and how), prepare a worksheet or small practical activity to achieve a confident level.

Class Work

1. Warm-up and Objective

- Introduce the students to the idea of conversation starters.
- Introduce the main topic of the lesson chosen in the teacher's preparation work.
- Introduce a (5W+H) question activity if the students need it.
- Talk about the final goal of the lesson: to start a conversation and keep it going using connecting questions, and to use the 5W+H question forms appropriately.

2. Exploration and Comprehension

- First, start by writing the topic on the board. Don't include the questions yet.
- On a piece of paper, students should draw an oval in the middle of the page. It should be big enough to fit the topic word and have room to write many more words outside it.
- The class should now brainstorm the topic. Create small groups of around 3 or 4 students within the class.
- After 5-10 minutes, ask questions about the topic. In addition, ask what students initially thought about the topic and why the students chose the words they did.

- Now is a good time to introduce the preliminary questions. This can introduce areas the students didn't initially cover.
- To start the conversations, clear the board and write down the left-hand side four connecting subject words the teacher thinks are the best for expanding on. Leave large spaces between for further words.
- Next, students will give related words based on one of the new words. Aim for two words per subject. Simply draw two short diagonal lines away from the first word to connect to students' answers. Upon completion, there should be eight new words in column 2.
- Again, divide the words in the second column so as to have two more diagonal lines with two new words connecting to the previous word. This time there will be 16 new words in column 3.

3. Guided Student Practical
- After completing the three columns, students should write eight sentences

using any combination of three words
from the board.
- It's important to obtain a proper sentence -
  students shouldn't use any words
  together that they feel like.
- Upon completion, ask the students to
  compare and proof their sentences in
  pairs. This should include the other
  student asking questions about the
  statement given. For examples of basic
  questions, refer to the sample questions
  for the subject chosen in teacher's
  preparation.

4. Student Presentation and Evaluation

- After proofing their sentences, ask each
  student in turn to share a sentence for
  the teacher to write on the board.
- Depending on how many students there
  are, ask students to give more sentences.
- Continue with more questions from other
  students about the sentences.

5. Review and Assess

- After a while of sentences building up on
  the board, ask students why they chose

the words that they did. This is to question their understanding.
- Ask for questions using the main question forms, from other students about a sentence given. Students should have built up their confidence from the questions in the previous practical pair work.

Bonus Activity

The Biggest Word List Game
- Students should write as many words in connection with a given category, for example, "fruit."
- After 5-10 minutes, ask the students to stop writing.
- Next, go around the class asking individual students for their words. Each student stands up and speaks each word aloud.
- If any other student has the same word then they scratch it off their list, including the speaker.
- Keep going and test everyone's word lists.
- When everyone has finished, ask students to count the remaining words on their lists.

- The winner is the person who has the largest total.

References

Below are a number of topics with activities relating to each one. For each activity four questions are listed.

Countries

- Cities - Which city in this country do you like the most? What items can we find in a city? What city did you grow up in? What are the differences between the cities in your country and in this country?
- Countries - What countries do you like? Where have you visited? What countries are your neighbours/neighbors? Where would you like to visit one day?
- Nationalities - What is a nationality? Can you describe the typical characteristics of your nation's people? Which nationalities do you like the most? Which other nationalities have you met?
- Transportation - What types of transportation do you know? What kind of vehicle can you drive or ride? What is the purpose of different types of

transportation? What is your
favourite/favorite type of car?

- Travel - Where have you
travelled/traveled? Why have you
travelled/traveled? What do you think of
other cultures? Do you live with foreign
influences?

Education

- Books - What books have you read? What
books do you have plans to read later?
What genres of books do you know?
Have you ever read a book because of a
film/movie?
- Classroom - What would you usually expect
to see in a classroom? What items
shouldn't be in a classroom? Should we
use technology? What should a perfect
classroom be like?
- Future - What will you do in the future?
What do you do now to plan your future?
What do you predict for the future?
What do you wish will be invented in the
future?
- History - What history do you know about?
What time in history would you like to
have seen? Do you agree that now is the

best time to live? What would you like to be famous for in history?

- School - What did you enjoy studying the most? Who was your favourite/favorite teacher? Did/Do you ever skip school? Were there ever any problems at school?
- Space - What is in space? Can you name some stars and planets? Would you like to travel in space? Do you believe in aliens?
- Study - How do you like to study? What techniques are the best to do well in tests? What do you want to study later in life? What do you find easy to learn?
- Technology - What is technology? What technology do you own? What do you think will happen in 10 or 20 years with phones and computers? Is technology good or bad for us?

Environment

- Animals - What animals do you like? What types of animals can you name? What type of animals do you know? What do you think of zoos?
- Birds - What birds do you know? What birds have you seen? Do you know what

a bird of prey is? What proof is there that dinosaurs are the ancestors of birds?

- •Nature - What is nature? What nature have you seen? Have you experienced a natural disaster? How can we help to protect nature?
- •Pets - What is a pet? What pets have you had? What animal would you like as a pet? What do you think about having dangerous pets?
- •Recycle - What is recycling? How do you recycle? What do you think of pollution? How can we make recycling better?
- •Weather - What is weather? How has the weather been recently? What is your idea of perfect weather? Where were you the last time the weather was terrible?

Hobbies

- •Art - What is art? Can you make art? Do you like all types of art? What art would you like at home?
- •Cooking - Do you like cooking? What can you cook? What instruments do you like to use in the kitchen? Have you ever had a cooking disaster?

- Driving - Have you driven before? What would you like to drive? Are roads safe? What will future cars look like?
- Films/movies - What are some film/movie genres? What is a good film/movie? Who works to make a film/movie? Can you name a famous actor?
- Food - What foods do you like and dislike? Where does your food come from? Have you ever grown food? How much does your food cost?
- Games - What games do you play now? What type of games do you know? What games can you remember from last year? What games can you never play well?
- Gardening - Do you like gardening? What plants are in your house? Have you ever grown vegetables? What types of plants do you know?
- Music - What are some music genres? Which music do you like? What music do you not like? Can you sing?
- Shopping - Where do you go shopping? If you were rich, what would you buy? What snacks do you like to buy? Do you look for bargains?
- Sport - What sports do you watch? What sports can you play? Have you ever won

a medal? Do you prefer single or team sports?

Personal

- Body - How healthy are you? Have you ever broken a bone? Do you compare yourself to others? What would you change about your appearance?
- Emotions - What are emotions? How do you generally feel? What changes your emotions? How do you make yourself feel better?
- Exercise - Do you like exercise? When was the last time you went to a gym? Why do we need exercise? Is exercise enough on its own to make us healthy?
- Happy - What is happiness? What makes you happy? Do you buy goods to make you happy? How often are you unhappy?
- Memory - How good is your memory? How easy is it for you to study? Have you ever forgotten a bag? How can we improve our memory?
- Morality and Ethics - What are morals? Where do they come from? What would you do in a difficult situation? Do you like other people's actions and thinking?

People

- Celebrations - When do you have celebrations? When was your most memorable celebration? Why do we celebrate? Have you always enjoyed being with your family?
- Family - What family traits do you have? Who do you follow in your family? Can you describe a family member? When was the last time all of your family were together?
- Home - How long have you lived where you are now? Where was your childhood home? Do you like to change homes? What would be your dream home?
- People - How would you describe your country's people? What is culture? What cultures do you know about? How do you feel being in another country?
- Relationships - What is a relationship? Are all relationships good? What makes a best friend? Where are good places to make new relationships?
- Role Model - What is a role model? Do you have a role model? Are you a role model to others? How can we be a role model?

Social

- Communication - What is communication? Where do you communicate? How do you communicate? How much technology do you use to communicate?
- Controversy - What subjects are controversial? When does controversy happen? Why does controversy occur? What can be done to prevent it?
- Crime - What is crime? Have you ever witnessed a crime? What is done to combat crime? Why do we need the law?
- Jobs - What jobs can you describe? What is your ideal job? Why would you like to do a certain job? What jobs would you not do?
- Money - Where do you spend your money? How do you save money? Do hobbies cost you money? When do you want to retire?
- Politics - What is politics? Do you follow politics? What is your opinion about politicians? Have you ever voted?
- Television - What do you watch on TV? Do you watch English programmes/programs? What genres do you like? How much TV do you watch?

- Working - What is work? Where have you worked or would like to work? What do you need to do at work? What work would you not want to do?

Expanding Vocabulary

Purpose

This lesson focuses on expanding vocabulary with synonyms and antonyms. This is a fun lesson that encourages open speaking and explores the use of verbs in depth. This is then used to build dialogue with simple questions and answers.

Example

Ownership: Have - I have a new car. How much did it cost?

Lesson

Objectives

1. To expand the use of common verbs with questions and answers.
2. To use synonyms and antonyms for selected verbs.

Teacher Preparation

1. Choose a verb from References at the end of this lesson, for example, "Ownership: Have - I have a new car. How much did it cost?"
2. Choose three antonyms and three synonyms related to the verb chosen for comprehension checking.
3. Find some pictures closely related to the subject (in this case, "Ownership"). These could be computer printouts, cards or a PowerPoint presentation.
4. Students will need mini-whiteboards and whiteboard markers for part 4 (the quiz).
5. Make small cards (about 12-20). These are simply playing cards with an "F" (for False) or a "T" (for True) on them. This is

for the bonus activity and is therefore
optional.

Class Work

1. Warm-up and Objective

- Introduce the concepts of synonyms and
  antonyms and check that the students
  understand the meaning of each.
- Introduce the main subject of the lesson
  chosen in the teacher's preparation work.
- Talk about the final goal of the lesson: to
  understand the difference between
  synonyms and antonyms and to expand
  the use of common verbs with questions
  and answers.

2. Exploration and Comprehension

- Write the verb on the board and ask for an
  example statement and answer.
- If this is difficult, use the sample statement
  and question given in the Reference
  section for the verb chosen.
- Ask if the students can elaborate any
  potential situations.

- Discuss the subject together in class. Write down any ideas students suggest and discuss further.
- Introduce the pictures from teacher's preparation work and discuss them also.
- Draw a two-column table on the board and label the columns "Synonyms" and "Antonyms."
- Start by asking for synonyms and antonyms connected to the initial verb chosen and write them in the correct column.
- Go over the new verbs given and again ask briefly, for example, "statements and questions."

3. Guided Student Practical

- Divide the students into teams or pairs (depending on the class size). They will use synonyms and antonyms to create statements and questions based around the selected verb.
- The number of statements depends on how many teams there are and how much time is available for the quiz.

- The statements generated by students must include synonyms and antonyms derived from the initial verb.

4. Student Presentation and Evaluation

- The groups will now come together for a class quiz using the material produced earlier.
- The quiz is aimed at guessing the other groups' new synonym or antonym.
- The first group reads aloud one of the statements and questions what the students thought of. They need to make sure to leave a gap where their new verb should be.
- The other groups write down their guess on their mini-boards.
- Points are awarded for correct answers and logged for each group.

5. Review and Assess

- Continue with the game while the students are contributing, then if there is time, switch to the bonus activity.

Bonus Activity

Find the Lie

- This game runs with the intention of convincing others that everyone is telling the truth. However, three of the team are telling the truth and one is telling a lie.
- The game starts with two teams of four students.
- Each student has one of the four cards (written "T", "T", "T" and "F").
- The team has a couple of minutes to come up with a sentence for each of the four students, for example, "I've never eaten meat" or "I can speak three languages." They can write the sentences down if needed.
- After completing their sentences the students are ready to reveal them to the other team.
- The guessing team can ask only five questions to find out who is telling the truth.
- After the five questions the guessing team should choose who is telling the lie.
- If the students find the lie they are the winner.

- If there is a large class, create many groups of four students and rotate their turns at being each team.

References

Below are numerous common verbs categorized by topic. For each verb, an introductory sentence and responding question are listed.

Ability

- Build - I will build a new table. Where will you put it?
- Change - I want to change this shirt. Is there a problem?
- Cut - I want to cut this tree down. Is it dangerous?
- Feel - It feels like rain. Will the weather get worse?
- Hear - I can hear something. Yes, what is it?
- Help - I might be able to help you. Thanks, can you hold this here?
- Let - I cannot let you watch TV. What is wrong with TV?
- Make - I will make a birthday cake. Who is it for?
- Meet - I will meet my boss later. What will the meeting be about?
- Play - I can play golf. How good are you?

- Reach - I cannot reach the cookie jar. Would you like to use this chair?
- Sit - Please sit in this chair. Thanks. Who will sit next to me?
- Stand - My back is hurting, I need to stand up. Are you OK?
- Try - I would like to try fishing. Me too. Let's plan a trip sometime.
- Use - I would like to use those pens, please. Sure. How about these too?
- Work - I work at an expensive restaurant. What is your job?
- Write - I like to write stories. Can I read some, please?

Looking

- Find - I cannot find my watch. Where was it last?
- Look - Look, my friend is coming. What is he/she wearing?
- Read - I like to read sci-fi. Who is your favourite/favorite author?
- See - I can see a taxi. Is it our car?
- Show - Let me show you how to use this. When did you learn to do that?
- Watch - I like to watch films/movies. What is your favourite/favorite film/movie?

Mind

- Allow - I cannot allow you in this room. Why is that room closed?
- Believe - I believe in aliens. Have you ever seen one?
- Know - I know how to drive a car. Can you show me?
- Learn - I want to learn how to play the guitar. I can show you if you like.
- Like - I like strawberry ice cream. Sorry, it's all gone. Would you like another flavour/flavor?
- Love - I love cheese pizzas. Hmm, yes. Shall we get some?
- Remember - I cannot remember my password. What is your password clue?
- Seem - It seems I arrived too early. Can you help us with the chairs?
- Think - I think we are lost. Do you have a map?
- Understand - I cannot understand how to use this. Can I help with that?

Moving

- Come - Come here please. Am I in trouble?
- Get - I can get a better picture over there. Would you like me to move?

- Go - If you take that road we'll get there quicker. Yes, but are there any parking spaces?
- Leave - I would like to leave this company. What, is it something I said?
- Move - We will move house next week. Where will you move?
- Open - I'll open this door for you. Thanks, can you open that one too?
- Run - I had to run to catch the bus. Did you catch it?
- Stay - I would like to stay in this restaurant, but it's too noisy. Where shall we go?
- Walk - I had to walk to work today. Ah, did you have an umbrella?

Ownership

- Bring - I can bring some food. Great! What should I bring?
- Give - I give great advice at work. How did you help there?
- Have - I have a new car. How much did it cost?
- Hold - I am holding a big box. What is inside?
- Keep - I would like to keep all these books. May I borrow one?

- Offer - I would like to offer 1000 pounds/dollars for your car. That's great, but how about 2000 pounds/dollars?
- Provide - I can provide snacks. What snacks do you have?

Speaking

- Ask - I asked my teacher for more homework. Are you struggling at school?
- Call - Please call me when you arrive in France. It might be early, is that OK?
- Say - I can say this hotel looks amazing. Yes, have you seen the bathroom?
- Speak - I can speak three languages. Do you like to study?
- Talk - I will have to talk to the manager. Is there a problem?
- Tell - Please tell me how you made this food. Gladly. Do you like it?

Timing

- Become - I would like to become a better person. What would you like to change?
- Begin - I will begin with cleaning the windows. Do you have a spare sponge?
- Continue - I would like to continue reading this book later. Is it a good book?

- Start - Please start the test now. How long do we have?
- Stop - Stop making that noise. Sorry, are you angry?
- Wait - Wait here, I'll be back with a gift. What is the occasion?

Wish/Want

- Buy - I would like to buy oranges. Do you have a bag?
- Need - I need a box. How big a box do you need?
- Take - I will take these two books. Would you like anything else?
- Want - I want a new car. What type do you want?

Other Books

Since my initial ESL training and time spent teaching in South Korea, I have collected together some tried and tested lessons which I have transformed into a few books to help others with their lesson plans. For more information, check out the link below.

https://www.nigelmopenshaw.com/

Made in the USA
Monee, IL
05 December 2019